CONDUCTOR
08720666

DISCOVERY JAZZ
A Series For
Developing Jazz Ensemble

By BENNY GOLSON
KILLER JOE
Arranged by MICHAEL SWEENEY

TEACHING AIDS For The Director:

Benny Golson's classic jazz composition provides an excellent vehicle for teaching tempo and swing style. A good recorded version to have your students listen to is on the LP "QUINCY JONES: WALKING IN SPACE" which was recorded in 1969.

Be sure to work with your students to develop solid swing style 8th notes. Listening to the Quincy Jones recording and the enclosed soundsheet will help them understand the correct style to try to match. Insist that the tempo remains steady as the tendency will be to rush. In particular, the rhythm section should practice by themselves working on a solid tempo and good swing feel. The drummer should keep the patterns simple and concentrate on "time."

Use Unison Pattern B to work on uniformity and balance when playing the "fp." Throughout the arrangement, staccato quarter notes should be played in a separated manner but not too short.

The section at meas. 37 may be performed with a Saxophone soloist or as a Saxophone soli. Similarly, meas. 53 is a solo for any Trumpet or Trombone. This section may also be performed as a Trumpet and/or Trombone soli. Throughout the arrangement, the left hand in the piano part doubles the Bass part. This should be played only if there is no bass player available.

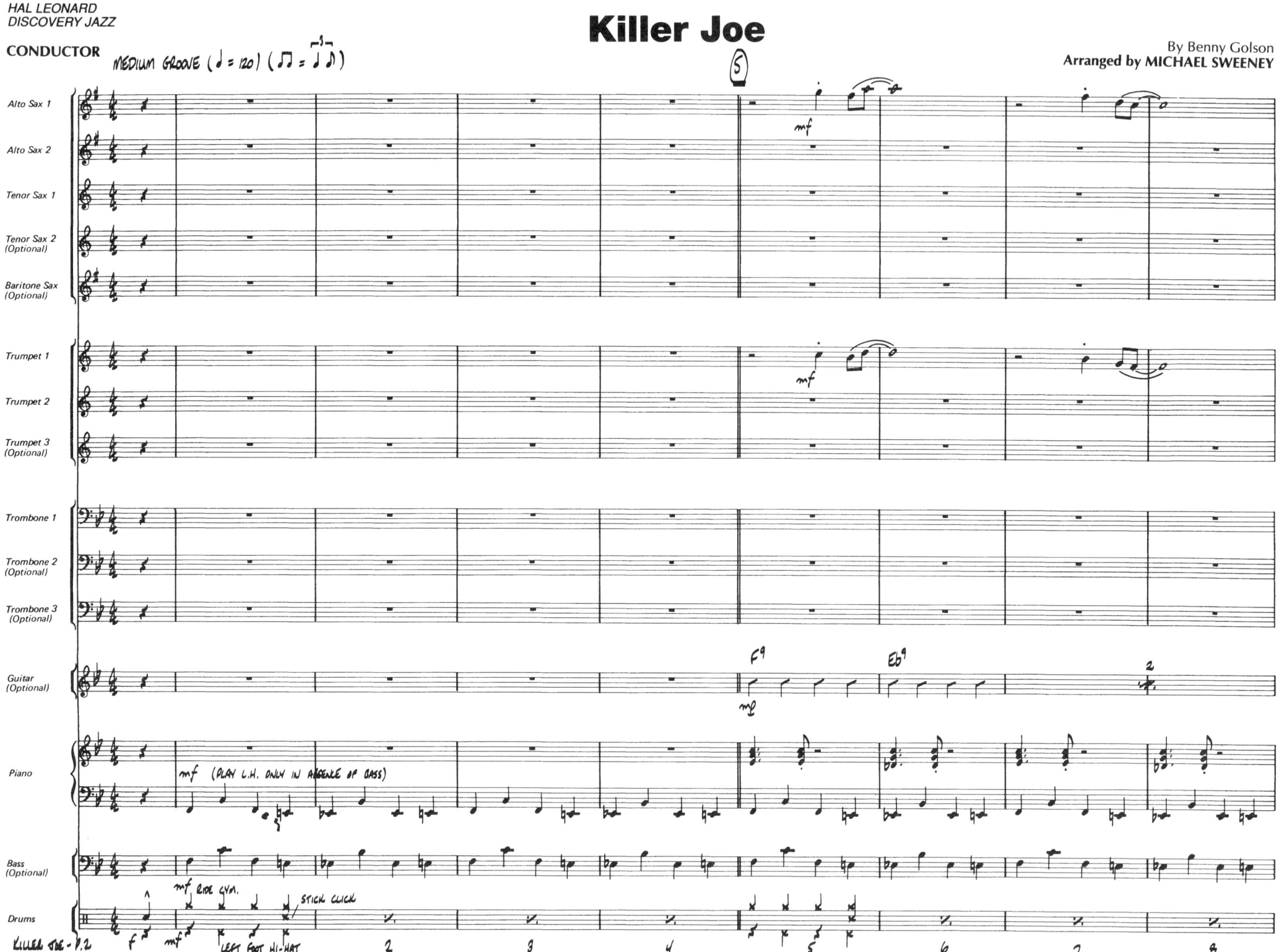

Killer Joe

HAL LEONARD DISCOVERY JAZZ

Alto Sax 2

By BENNY GOLSON
Arranged by MICHAEL SWEENEY

Killer Joe

HAL LEONARD DISCOVERY JAZZ

TRUMPET 1

By BENNY GOLSON
Arranged by MICHAEL SWEENEY

Copyright © 1959 Time Step Music
Copyright Renewed 1987 Time Step Music
This arrangement Copyright © 1989 Time Step Music
All rights for Time Step Music administered by Mayflower Music Corporation
International Copyright Secured   Made in U.S.A.   All Rights Reserved

HAL LEONARD
DISCOVERY JAZZ

Killer Joe

Trombone 1

By BENNY GOLSON
Arranged by MICHAEL SWEENEY

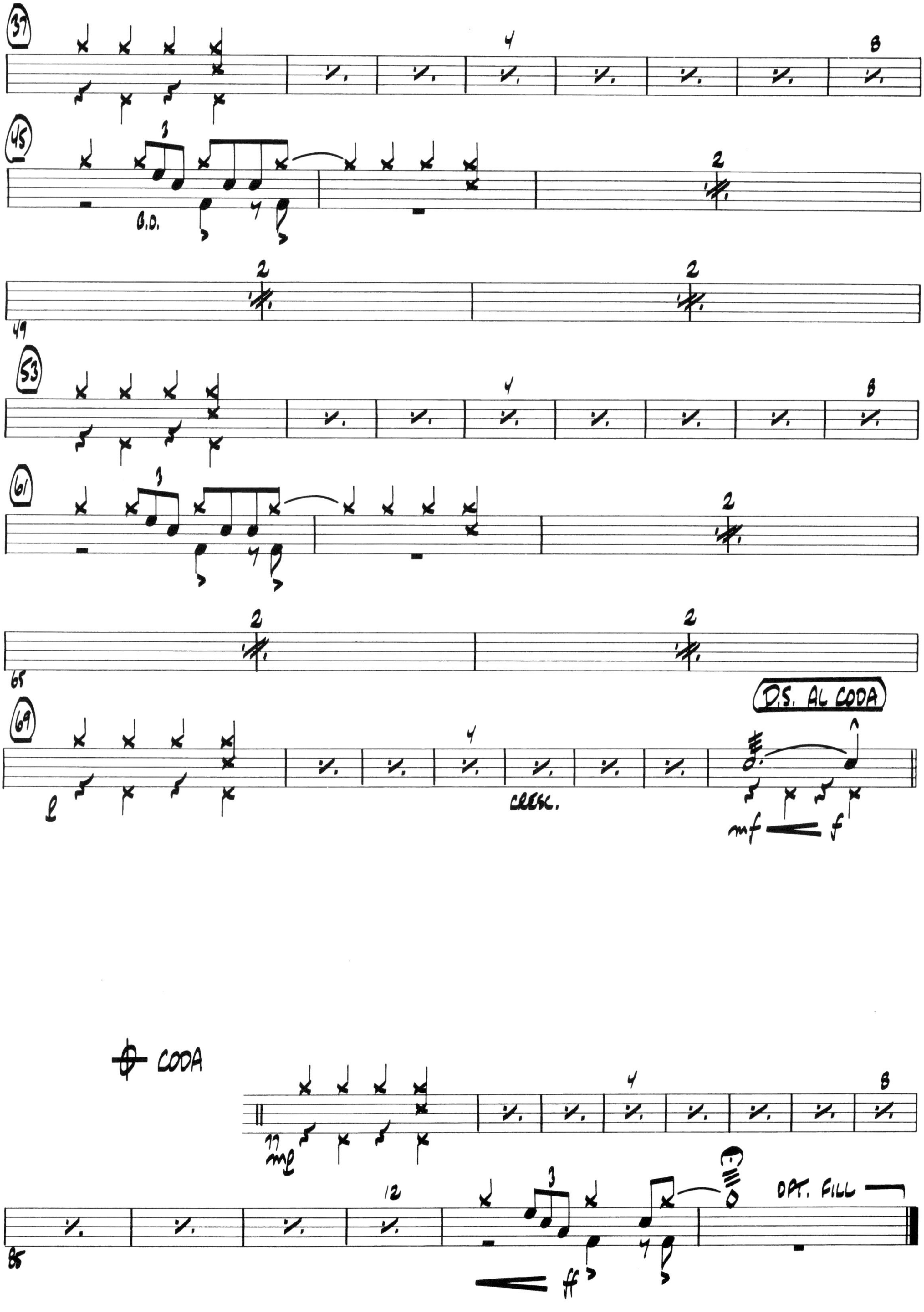
37
45
B.D.
49
53
61
65
69
D.S. AL CODA
CRESC.
mf
f
CODA
77
mp
85
OPT. FILL
ff

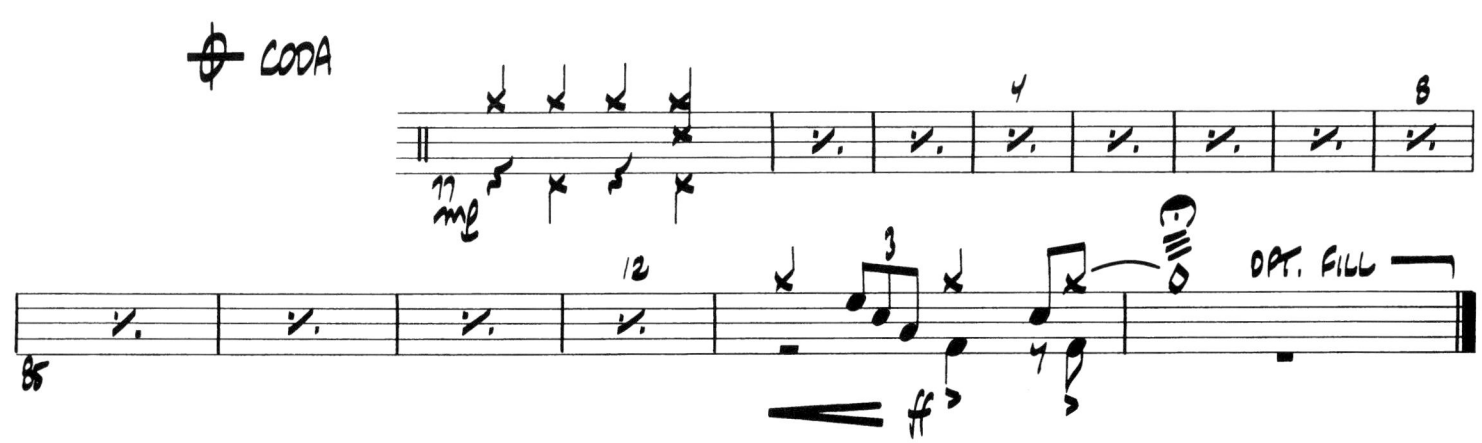

HAL LEONARD
DISCOVERY JAZZ

Killer Joe

PIANO

By BENNY GOLSON
Arranged by MICHAEL SWEENEY

UNISON PATTERNS

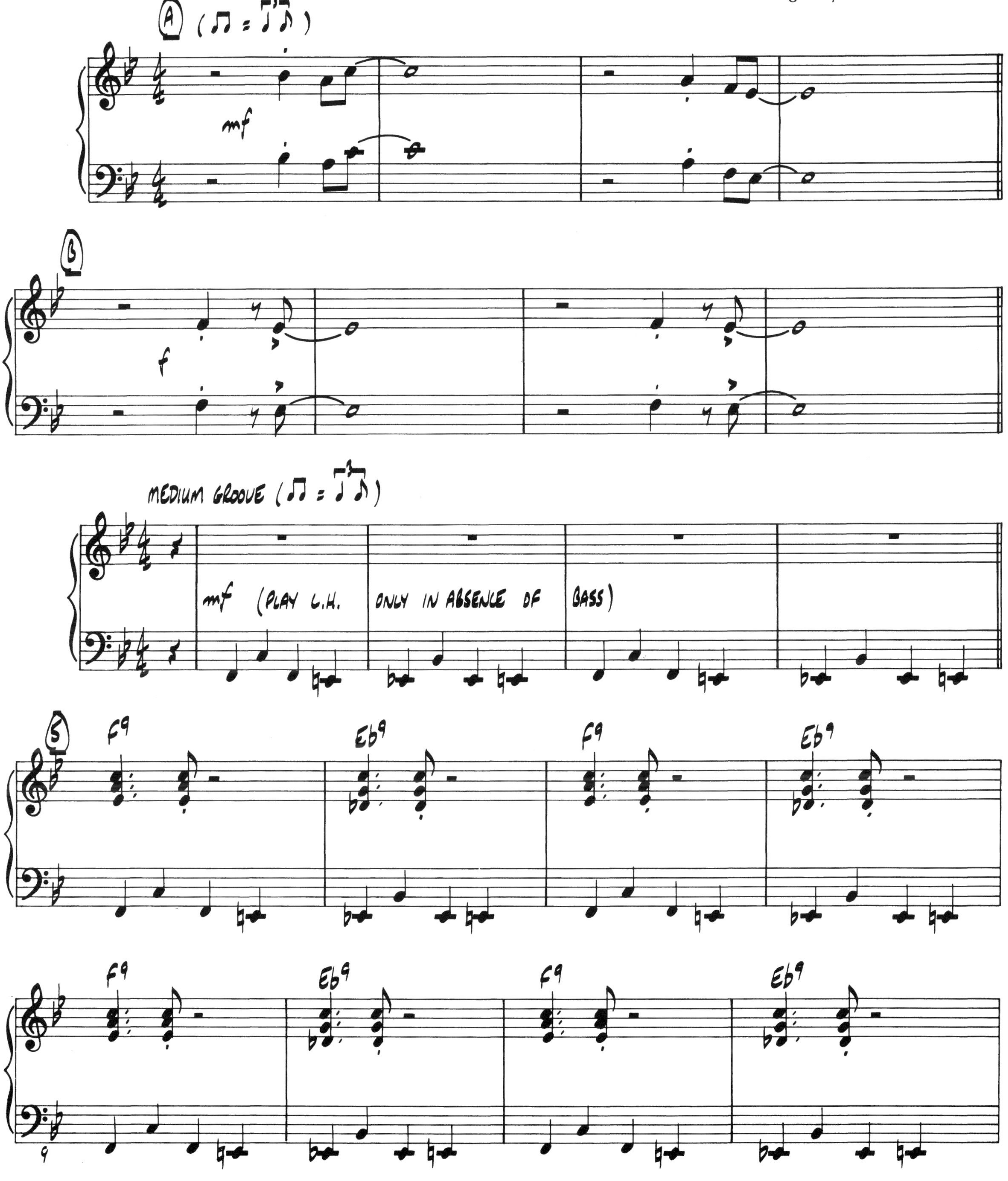